AN ACCOUNT OF THE MANNERS OF THE GERMAN INHABITANTS OF PENNSYLVANIA, WRITTEN 1789

METALMARK BOOKS

Yours truly

I. D. Rupp,

AN ACCOUNT

OF THE

MANNERS

OF THE

GERMAN INHABITANTS

OF PENNSYLVANIA,

WRITTEN 1789,

BY

BENJAMIN RUSH, M. D.

NOTES ADDED

BY

PROF. I. DANIEL RUPP,

Author, Translator, Member of the Historical Society
of Pennsylvania; Hon. Mem. Minnesota His. Soc.; Hon.
Mem. His. Soc. of Wisconsin; Cor. Mem. of the N. Eng.
His. and Genealogical Soc.; Hon. Mem. Phrenakos-
mian Soc. Pa. Coll.; Hon. Mem. Moravian His. Soc.
of Nazareth; Deigmadedachian Soc. of the Theol.
Sem. Gettysburg; Hon. Mem. of the Diagno-
thian Lit. Soc. Marshall Coll; Cor. Mem.
York Co. Cabinet of Nat. Sciences and
Lyceum; Mem. of Swatara Lit. Inst.;
Ehren Mitglied Des Deutschen Pi-
oniers Verein, Cincinnati, O.

PUBLISHED BY

SAMUEL P. TOWN,

614 CHESTNUT ST.

PHILADELPHIA.

1875.

PREFACE.

BENJAMIN RUSH, M. D., the *Author of the Account of the Manners of the German Inhabitants, of Pennsylvania,* was a native of· Pennsylvania, born December 24, 1745, at Bristo!, Bucks County. He was educated at Princeton College, N. J. Studied Medicine in Philadelphia, London, Edinburg and Paris. In 1769, was made Professor of Chemistry, in the Philadelphia Medical College, and became a contributor to Medical Literature. He was elected a member of the Continental Congress; he advocated and signed the Declaration of Independence. In 1777, he was appointed Surgeon-general and Physician-general, of the Continental army. His duties did not prevent him from writing a series of letters on the Constitution of Pennsylvania, which was changed by his influence. He resigned his post in the army, because he could not prevent frauds upon soldiers in the hospital stores.

In 1785, he planned the Philadelphia Dispensary, the first in the United States; and was a member of the convention, which ratified the Federal Constitution. Retiring from politics, he became Professor of the Theory and Practice of Medicine, in Philadelphia Medical College ; and was so successful in the treatment of yellow fever, 1793, that he was believed to have saved the lives of 6,000 persons. His practice, in consequence, became so large that he prescribed for one hundred patients a day, whom he saw, even at his meals. His Medical works produced honors from several European Sovereigns. In 1799, he was appointed Treasurer of the United States Mint, which post he held until his death, in Philadelphia, April 19, 1813.

He was one of the greatest and best men that have adorned his country. Few men have been greater ornaments to their country than *Dr Rush;* and, very few, indeed, had acquired a greater reputation, both at home and abroad. He was a beneficent philanthropist and an exemplary christian. *Thatcher's Med. Biog., Chamber's Ency. Davenport.*

AN ACCOUNT

OF THE

MANNERS OF THE GERMAN INHABITANTS

OF PENNSYLVANIA.

THE State of Pennsylvania is so much indebted for her prosperity and reputation, to the *German* part of her citizens,* that a short *Account* of

-----

* Governor George Thomas, of the Province of Pennsylvania, wrote to the Bishop of Exeter, England, April 23, 1747. "The Germans of Pennsylvania, are, I believe, *three-fifths* of the whole population, (*whole population*, 200,000). They have, by their industry, been the principal instruments of raising the state to its present flourishing condition, beyond any of his Majesty's Colonies, in North America."

Papers relating to the History of the Episcopal Church, in Pennsylvania, by W. S. Perry, D. D., p. 265.

Pennsylvania took the lead of all the colonial states in agriculture, because of the many German settlers. In 1751, there were exported 86,000 bushels of wheat, 129,960 barrels of flour, 90,743 bushels of Indian corn. The total exports of 1751, exceeded in value, one million of dollars. I. D. R.

their *Manners* may, perhaps, be useful and agree-able to their fellow citizens in every part of the United States.

The aged Germans, and the ancestors of those who are young, emigrated chiefly from the Palàti-nate, from Alsace, Swabia, Saxony and Switzer-land : but natives of every principality and dukedom of Germany, are to be found in different parts of the state.* They brought but little property with them.† A few pieces of silver

---

* In *the Ship Lists*, the name *Palatines*, is indiscriminately applied to all imported Germans into Pennsylvania, prior to 1741 ; afterwards, they are designated, *Foreigners*, inhabitants of the *Palatinate*, and places adjacent ; Wittember-gers, from Erbach, foreigners from Wittemberg, Alsace, and Zweibruecken : from Nassau, Hanau, Darmstadt, Alsatians, Eisenberg, Basel, Swabia, Mannheim, Durlach, Rittenheim : inhabitants of Lorraine, Mentz, Franconia, Hesse, Hamburg, Saxony. After 1754, principalities, the duke-doms, districts, places or towns, are not desig-nated in the *Ship Lists*.

† Many who at home, had owned property, and converted it into money, were robbed in transitu, by ship owners, importers, sea captains, and Neulaender. The emigrants chests, with their clothes, and sometimes their money, were put on other vessels or ships, and left behind. These chests were rifled of their contents. The

coin or gold, a chest with clothes, a Bible and Prayer or Hymn book, constituted the whole stock of most of them.* Many of them bound themselves, or one or more of their children, to masters after their arrival, for four, five or seven

German immigrants thus treated, on their arrival at Philadelphia, were obliged to submit being sold as *Loskaeuflinge Redemptioners*, they and their children, to pay their passage money. In not a few cases, persons, who still had means, were held responsible to pay the passage for the poorer. This was the practice for more than fifty years. In this way, persons of substance were necessitated, and did become, very frequently, common beggars. *Col. Rec. IV. 586, Penna. Arch IV. 472. Gordon's History of Penna. p. 300.*

* If they were German Reformed, they brought with them, also, the Heidelberg Catechism; and a few of them, the Palatinate Liturgy, of 1684. In 1731, there were 15,000 German Reformed members, in Penna., from the Palatinate, and from the districts of Nassau, Waldeck, Witgenstein and Wetterau. *Harbaugh's Lifes of the Ger. Ref, church Fathers,* I. p. 226.

If the immigrants were Lutherans, they brought with them, Luther's Catechism, Arndt's Wahre's Christenthum. The Augsburg Confession of faith. The Lutheran membership did not exceed 17,000 in 1731.

years,* to pay for their passages across the ocean.
A Clergyman always accompanied them, when
they came in large bodies.†

---

* The usual terms of sale, depended somewhat,
on the age, strength and health of the persons
sold.   Boys and girls, usually had to serve from
five to ten years, till they attained the age of
twenty-one.   Many parents were necessitated, as
they had been wont at home, to do with their
cattle, *sell their own children.*   The children had
to assume the passage money, of both their own,
and that of their parents, in order that the latter
might be released from the ship.   Children under
five years of age, could not be sold.   They-were
disposed of gratuitously, to such persons as agreed
to raise them, and let them go free when they
attained the age of twenty-one.

It was an humble position that Redemptioners
occupied.   " Yet, says Gordon, from this class have
sprung some of the most reputable and wealthy
inhabitants of this province."   Gordon's His. Pa.
p. 556.

In the years 1728, '29, '37, '41, '50 and 1751,
large numbers of *Redemptioners,* or those who
bound themselves, came to Pennsylvania.   Prior
to 1727, most of the Germans commigrated and
were persons of means.   Loeher, p. 80.

See An original Fire-side His.

† The *Rev. George Michael Weis,* V. D. M., a
native of the Palatinate, on the Rhine, a German
Reformed minister, who graduated at Heidelberg,
came to Pennsylvania in a company with about
400 emigrants, natives and inhabitants, of the

The principal part of them, were farmers,* but there were many machanics, who brought with

---

Palatinate. They arrived in Philadelphia, Sept. 21, 1727, in the ship William and Sarah, Revd. Weis was a learned divine. Rev. Andrews, in a letter, to the Rev. Prince, of Boston, Oct. 14, 1730, speaks of Weis "as a bright young man and a fine scholar, he speaks Latin, as readily as we do our vernacular tongue." *Hazard's Reg. of Pa., XV. p.* 198.

Rev. Weis, announced through the *American Weekly Mercury,* Phila., Feb. 3, 1729-30, that he would teach Logic, Natural Philosophy, Metaphysics, &c., to all, such as were willing to learn. Weis died. 1763. He is buried in the church, at New Goshenhoppen, Montgomery County, Pa. *Rupp's collection of* 30,000 *Names, p.* 6. *Harbaugh's Fathers of the Ger. Ref. church, I. pp.* 265-274.

The *Rev. Johann Casper Stoever,* Missionary, and his son, Johann Casper Stoever, S. S. Theol. stud. with ninety Palatines, arrived at Phila. in the ship James Goodwill, in Sept. 1728. Mr. Stoever was born in Strasburg, Germany—was for many years, pastor of the Lutheran church, at Lebanon—he died near that place, May 13, 1779, aged, 71 years, 3 months and 2 days. Many of his descendants still reside in Pennsylvania. *Col.* 30,000 *Names, p.* 13.

* "The Germans," says Proud, "seem more adapted to agriculture and improvement of a wilderness; and the Irish, for trade. The Germans soon get estates in this country, where industry and economy are the chief requisites to procure them." *Proud's His. of Pa.* II. 274.

them, a knowledge of those arts which are necessary and useful in all countries.* These mechanics were chiefly weavers, tailors, tanners, shoemakers, comb-makers, smiths of all kinds, butchers, paper-makers, watch-makers, sugar-bakers.†

---

* At the close of the term of apprenticeship, the young mechanic, before he was allowed to set up for himself, was obliged, according to the custom of Guilds and Trades, in Germany, to make his *Wanderschaft, Peregrination* of one or more years, in order to perfect himself in his trade; and, he had to show some well finished piece of workmanship, before he could be promoted to the honor of master-workman, in any town, except where he was raised.

The *Wanderschaft* custom, if properly improved, afforded opportunities to acquire, besides a proficiency in their trade, much useful knowledge in general, which books alone, could not supply. For the intention of this custom, was, that the *Handwerks-Bursch Travelling Journeyman* should gain experience in his craft, and learn methods practised in the countries, besides his own, as well as some knowledge of the world. It is nothing unusual to meet, in Germany, with common mechanics, who speak three or four different languages, well informed as to the state of most of the countries of Europe, and possessing a general fund of knowledge, far superior to what is found in persons of the same class, in England. *Murray's Handbook*, p. 218.

† From the middle of April 1709, to the middle of July 1709, there arrived at London.

I shall begin this *Account* of the German Inhabitants of Pennsylvania, by describing the *Manners of the German Farmers.*

The Germans taken, as a body, especially as farmers, are not only industrious and frugal, but skilful cultivators of the earth. I shall enumerate a few particulars, in which they differ from most of the other farmers of Pennsylvania. (The *German's* farm was easily distinguished from those of others, by good fences, the extent of orchard, the fertility of soil, productiveness of

---

11,294 German Protestants—males and females— male occupations:—Husbandmen and Vine dressers, 1838; Bakers, 56; Masons, 87; Carpenters, 124; Shoemakers, 68; Tailors, 99; Butchers, 29; Millers, 45; Tanners, 14; Stocking weavers, 7; Barbers, 6; Locksmiths, 4; Cloth and Linen weavers, 95; Coopers, 82; Hunters, 7; Saddlers, 13; Glassblowers, 2; Hatters, 3; Lime-burners, 8; Schoolmasters, 18; Engravers, 2; Bakers, 22; Brickmakers, 3; Silversmiths, 2; Smiths, 35; Herds-men, 3; Blacksmiths, 48; Potters, 3; Turners, 6; Silversmiths, 2; Statuary, 1; Surgeons, 2; Masons, 39.

Of the 11,294 emigrants, 2,556 had families. *Kapp,* 89, 90——*Frankfurter-Mess-Kalender von Ostern bis Herbst,* 1709, *pa.* 90.

See Appendix A. An Original Fireside History of German and Swiss Immigrants, in Pennsylvania, from 1682 to 1765, by I. D. Rupp.

the fields, the luxuriance of the meadows. *Co-lum-Mag. for* 1790, I. D. R.)

First. In settling a tract of land, they always provide large and suitable accomodations for their horses and cattle, before they lay out much money in building a house for themselves. The barn and the stables, are generally under one roof, and contrived in such a manner, as to enable them to feed their horses and cattle, and to remove their dung, with as little trouble as possible.

The first dwelling house upon this farm, is small, and built of logs.* It generally lasts the life time of the first settler, of a tract of land; and hence, they have a saying, that "a son

---

* A house built by a German, could, even at a distance, be readily distinguished from one erected by a Scotch, Irish or Englishman. Had the house but one chimney, and this in the middle, (*in der Mitte des Hauses,*) then it was a German's. They had stoves. To economise in the use of stove pipes, the chimney occupied the central portion. A house with a chimney at each gable end, was erected by an Englishman. *Schoepf's Reise durch Pennsylvanien,* 1783, p. 185.

If there was a spring on his farm, which supplied him with water, he built a milk house, and, on the floor above, was a place to smoke meat, if not, a loft to store winter apples. I. D. R.

should always begin his improvements, where his father left off," that is, by building a large and convenient stone house.

Second. They always prefer good land, or that land on which there is a large quantity of meadow ground.* From an attention to the cultivation of grass, they often double the value of an old farm in a few years, and grow rich on

---

* " The Germans, wisely chose some of the best land in the state, where they soon made themselves comfortable, and next grew quietly rich. * * * The German population of Pennsylvania, naturally increasing, and augmented by continual accessions from the Fatherland, has since spread over a large portion of the State, still inheriting the economy and prudent foresight of their ancestors, and generally establishing themselves on the most fertile soils." *Trego*, p. 84.

The Germans have supplanted, in many counties, the Scotch Irish. Cumberland, originally settled by Scotch Irish, has now a prevailingly German population. In Northampton county,, though there was at first a moiety of Irish or Scotch Irish settlers ; *now*, nine-tenths of the inhabitants are Germans. As early as 1790, Germans to the number of 145,000 were scattered through the State. Five-sixths of East Pennsylvania, are Germans. In the city of Philadelphia, Reading and Lancaster, and the towns of Germantown, Allentown, Easton, &c., we find many Germans. I. D. R.

farms, on which their predecessors of whom they
purchased them, had nearly starved. They prefer purchasing farms with improvements, to settling on a new tract of land. [*Gypsum*, or
sulphate of lime, was used as a fertilizer, by
Germans. Jacob Berger, a German, was the first
that tried *gypsum*, several years before the Revolutionary war, on a city lot, on the commons of
Philadelphia. *Memoirs of Agricul. Socty.* Vol. I.
p. 156.]

Third. In clearing new land, they do not
girdle or belt* the trees simply, and leave them

---

* The process of *girdling or belting*, was, to
chop entirely around the tree, a curve of three or
four inches wide. A tree was not well deadened
unless it was cut to the red—cut completely
through the *alburnum* or sap. Seventy years
ago, when a piece of land was cleared in Cumberland county, in the first place, it was staked
off by the *woodmen*, provided with a *Waldhacke*,
grub-ax, he would take up by the roots *die Bae-
umchen*, the saplings, which he could shake in
the root, by laying hold of the young tree, bend-
ing it backwards and forwards. If the roots
yielded to this action, it was called a *grub*. After
the land had been grubbed, the larger standing
sapplings, and trees were cut down, and chopped
into rail lengths, of eleven feet or cordwood lengths,
of four feet. The rail lengths were split for fenc-
ing purposes, the four feet lengths were split for

to perish in the ground, as is the custom of their English or Irish neighbors; but they generally cut them down and burn them. In destroying under-wood and bushes, they generally grub them out of the ground, by which means, a field is as fit for cultivation the second year after it is cleared, as it is in twenty years afterwards. The advantages of this mode of clearing, consist in the immediate product of the field, and in the greater facility with which it is plowed, harrowed and reaped. The expense of repairing a plow, which is often broken, is greater than the extraordinary expense of grubbing the same field completely, in clearing.*

---

fire wood. This done, the brush was picked into heaps, and when dry, fire was set to them. The clearing, *das gelichtete Stueck*, was then ready for the plow.

* Those who practiced *girdling or belting,* claimed, that thus deadning the timber, had its advantages—labor was saved in chopping down and burning the stuff on the ground. In some parts of Pennsylvania, it was impossible to cut down the timber, because farmers were too poor to pay for so much labor. The dead timber afforded fire wood for years, which obviated the necessity of resorting to the woods. When the deadened trees fell, the roots were taken out with the trees. In eight or ten years, the trees began to fall

Fourth. They feed their horses and cows well, of which they keep only a small number, in such a manner, that the former perform twice the labor of those horses, and the latter yield twice the quantity of milk of those cows, that are less plentifully fed.* There is great economy in this practice, especially in a country where so much of the labor of a farmer is necessary to support his domestic animals. A German horse is known

---

rapidly. When the ground was pretty well covered with old logs, the farmer commenced "to *nigger-off*," which was effected by laying the broken limbs and smaller trees across the logs and putting fire to it. The young members of the family, *boys and girls,* followed to *chunck up* the fires. In a few days, the logs were *niggered-off,* at the length of 12 or 15 feet. Sometimes the entire tree was consumed. When the logs were thus reduced to lengths, that they could be handled by a few men, the owner had a *log-rolling.* He invited some of his neighbors, who assembled to aid him in his *rolling.* Usually, at such rollings, not a little hilarity prevailed, by reason of the free use of the German's *Branntwein,* the Irishman's *uisge-beatha, usquebaugh,* the Frenchman's, *Eau de vie,* water-of-life. I. D. R.

* It is a maxim with Germans: Mit Futtern ist Keine Zeit verloren, i. e. To feed well, no time is lost. Wer gut futtert-gut buttert, i. e. He that feeds well, churns much butter. I. D. R.

in every part of the state; indeed, the *horse* seems to "feel with his lord, the pleasure and the pride" of his extraordinary size or fat.

Fifth. The fences (*die Zaeune*) of a German farm are generally high, and well built,* so that his fields seldom suffer from the inroads of his own, or his neighbors' horses, cattle, hogs or sheep.

Sixth. The German farmers are great economists of their *wood.* Hence, they burn it only in stoves, in which they consume but a 4th or 5th part of what is commonly burnt in ordinary open fire places; besides, their horses are saved by means of this economy, from that immense labour, in hauling wood in the middle of winter, which frequently unfits the horses of their (*Scotch*) neighbors for the toils of the ensuing spring. Their houses are, moreover, rendered so comfortable, at all times, by large close stoves,†

---

* Wie einer den Zaun haelt, haelt er auch das Gut, i. e. The condition of the fence, shows the condition of the farm. I. D. R.

† In some of their houses, the Germans used the *six-plate* stove, Christoph Saur, the printer, in Germantown, suggested the ten-plate stove, (S. died Sep. 25, 1758.) The ten-plate stove was cast at, or near Lancaster, Pa. In 1752, first came out the cannon stoves, made at Lancaster;

that twice the business is done by every branch of
the family, in knitting, spinning and mending
farming utensils, that is done in houses where
every member in the family crowds near a com-

---

and at Colebrookdale furnace, Berks Co. Pa.
They were used in churches and court rooms.
Watson's Annals, I. 218.

In some parts of Germany, porcelain stoves are
in use. The curious objects, of variegated colors,
white, cream and blue. A Tourists, who traveled
through Germany some eighteen years ago, says :
When we first saw *porcelain stoves* in hotels, by
the way, we thought they were movable closets
for china and other table furniture. In the room
where they stand, there is no sign of fire or door
for wood or coal, but they are adjusted to the
wall, and open into the hall, so that the same
chimney serves for the necessary masonry of any
number of stoves. We have seen them in places
twelve feet high, prettily ornamented, and furnished with shelves and niches for statues and
knicknacks. This one before, which we sit, is six
or eight feet high, and is raised a foot from the
floor, to allow space beneath for an aviary, which
contains some twenty or thirty canary birds,
who have a warm and equal temperature, and
hop about as merrily as if in their own sunny
clime * * * If we enter any twenty houses
at random, we shall see the same * * * The
stoves are made in different pieces, and baked
like other articles of potter's clay, and cemented
together. When whole, they are *veneered* with
a fine compound and painted * * * The ex-

mon fire-place, or shivers at a distance from it, with hands and fingures that move, by reason of the cold, with only half their usual quickness.

They discover economy in the preservation and increase of their wood, in several other ways. They sometimes defend it, by high fences, from their cattle; by which means, the young forest trees are suffered to grow, to replace those that are cut down for the necessary use of the farm. But where this cannot be conveniently done, they surround the stump of that tree which is most useful for fences, viz: the chestnut, with a small triangular fence. From this stump, a number of suckers shoot out in a few years; two or three of which in the course of five and twenty years, grow into trees of the same size as the tree from whose roots they derived their origin.

Seventh. They keep their horses and cattle as warm as possible, in winter,* by which means,

---

pense of the cheapest, is about twenty dollars. and of the finest, forty, fifty and sixty dollars. When once thoroughly warmed, they remain so half a day, and do not require such constant attention as those of iron, and give a more agreeable atmosphere. *Peasant Life in Germany,* p. 288.

* The German Proverb runs : Eine gute Kuh sucht man im Stalle i. e. One seeks for a good cow in the stable. I. D. R.

they save a great deal of their hay and grain;
for those animals when cold, eat much more than
when they are in a more comfortable situation.

Eight. The German farmers, live frugally in
their families, with respect to diet, furniture and
apparel.* They sell their most profitable grain,
which is wheat, and eat that which is less profitable, that is rye, or Indian corn. The profit to a
farmer, from this single article of economy, is
equal, in the course of a life time, to the price of
a farm for one of his children.

They eat sparingly, of boiled animal food, with
large quantities of vegetables, particularly sallad,
turnips, onions and cabbage, the last of which,
they make into *Sourcrout.*† They likewise use

---

* In an inventory of the goods of Andrew
Ferree, a wealthy farmer, of Lancaster Co., ap-
praised Nov., 24, 1735, the following articles are
enumerated, viz: A large Family Bible, £2;
two feather beds, £6; wearing clothes, £7;
sundry pewter, £2, 8 shillings; a box of iron,
4 shillings; sundry ironware, £2; a watering
pot, 6 shillings; wooden ware. £1; two iron pot
racks, £1; two chests, 15 shillings; spinning
wheel, 8 shillings; Total, £23, 1 shilling. I. D. R.

† *Sauer-Kraut,* is a wholesome food, if properly made, and not allowed to ferment beyond the
proper point. It had been, as some maintain,

a large quantity of milk and cheese in their diet. Perhaps the Germans do not proportion the quantity of animal food, to the degrees of their labour; hence, it has been thought, by some people, that they decline in strength sooner than their English or Irish neighbors. Very few of them use distilled spirits in their families; their common drinks are cider,* beer, wine and simple water.

---

among the favorite dishes upon the table of Charlemagne, (Karl der Grosse) king of France, who died, A. D. 814, and very likely was made by the Germans, of the days ot *Attila*, king of the Huns, who died, A. D. 453. Throughout Germany, it is served three or four times a week, during the winter. I. D. R.

* *Cider-making* among the early Germans. in Pennsylvania, was different from the present manner, which in days of yore, was quite unique. The apples were first pounded by a stamper in a trough or strong vessel used for that purpose, in a tub or barrel. After being thus bruised, the pumice was placed in a large split-basket, or a sort of *Kober*, (now written *Coover*), previously suspended to a limb of a tree, beneath which was placed a trough, by fastening together the edges of planks or boards, sawed or split, which served to catch and carry the juice, compressed by weights, usually stones, in the basket, into some vessel placed for its reception. Apple mills and cider presses were introduced between 1740 and 1745. I. D. R.

The furniture of their houses is plain and useful.
They cover themselves in winter, with light feather beds,* instead of blankets; in this contri-
vance, there is both convenience and economy,
for the beds are warmer than blankets, and they
are made by themselves. The apparel of the

---

* *Elkanah Watson* a New Englander, in a
tour from Providence, R. I. to South Carolina,
through Pennsylvania, in October 1777, says:
"*At Reamstown,* (Lancaster Co., Pa.,) I was
placed between two beds, without sheets or pillows.
This, as I was told, was a prevailing custom, but,
which, as far as my experience goes, tends little
to promote either the sleep or comfort of a
stranger." *Elkanah Watson's Men and Times,
&c..* p. 31.

A tourist writes from Toeplitz, a town and
watering place in Bohemia, 1831:—"At Berg-
grieshuebel, where we stopped for the night, we
were introduced for the first time, to the stewing
of a real *German bed.* It consists of two large
bags filled with downs, between which, without
any other covering, the luckless wight of a traveller is called to repose. How this *buttering on
both sides* may do in the winter, I shall not determine; but, heaven knows, that on the occasion
referred to, it was altogether insupportable. I
endeavored, but failed, to get a couch more in
unison with the atmosphere of summer, of course,
I was obliged, from sheer fatigue, to submit to
the dissolution and thaw of this fearful hot-bath."
Strang's Germany, p. 235

German farmers, is usually *home spun.** When they use European articles of dress, they prefer those of the best quality, and of the highest prices. They are afraid of debt, and seldom purchase anything without paying cash for it.

Ninth. The German farmers have large or profitable gardens near their houses. These contain little else but useful vegetables. Pennsylvania is indebted to the Germans, for the principal part of her knowledge in horticulture. There was a time when turnips and cabbage were the principal vegetables that were used in diet, by the citizens of Philadelphia.† This will not surprise

---

* The German farmer's motto is; Selbstgesponnen, selbst, gemacht: Rein dabei is Bauerntracht—Poetized.

To spin, to weave, to ready make his clothes,
And keep them clean, the frugal farmer knows.

Carpets, now deemed indispensaoie to comfort, were not to be seen in a German farmer's house, before 1800. There are still some Germans, especially among the *Amish* and *German Brethren,* who dispense with this comfort. Carpets were no where to be seen, in rooms or parlors, even in Philadelphia, till about 1750. I. D. R.

† During the Revolutionary war, some of the gardens in the vicinity of Philadelphia, were improved by German prisoners, who had been in the

those persons, who know that the first settlers in
Pennsylvania, left England, while horticulture was
in its infancy in that country. It was not till
the reign of William III, (who reigned from
1689—1702, I. D. R.) that this useful and agree-
able art was cultivated by the English nation.
Since the settlement of a number of German
gardners, in the neighborhood of Philadelphia,
the tables of all clases of citizens have been
covered with a variety of vegetables, in every
season of the year; and to the use of these vegetables, in diet, may be ascribed the general ex-
emption of the citizens of Philadelphia, from
diseases of the skin.

Tenth. The Germans seldom hire men to work
upon their farms. The feebleness of that authority which masters possess over *hired servants,**

---

service of the King of Great Britain—they introduced, and cultivated *broccoli,* turnip, cabbage, &c.
Schoepf, 136. I. D. R.

* Unlike their English and Irish neighors,
they never, as a general thing, had *colored* servants, or slaves. Berks, a German county, hav-
ing a population of 30,179, in 1790, had only 65
slaves in the *ratio* of *one* to 464 whites. Cumberland county, originally settled by Scotch-Irish,
with a pupulation in 1790, of 15,655, had 360
slaves, in the *ratio* of *one* to 44 whites. I. D. R.

is such, that their wages are seldom procured
from their labor, except in harvest, when they
work in the presence of their masters. The
wives and daughters of the German farmers,
frequently forsake, for a while, their dairy and
spinning-wheel, and join their husbands and
brothers, in the labour of cutting down, collect-
ing and bringing home, the fruits of the fields
and orchards. The work of the gardens is generally done by the women of the family.*

---

* Times and customs have changed since the
pristine settlements of Pennsylvania. Not more
than seventy years ago, the good house-wife aided
by her daughters, would cultivate the garden,
dress and keep it in order, decorate the cottage
with choice honeysuckles, direct the tendrils of
the native grape, that shaded the house. In the
winter, mothers and daughters spun flax; in the
spring, the wool, on the humming wheel: from
the warp and weft of the spun yarn, they wove
linnen, linsey and woolen webs. Then a loom
was found in every family. The linnen, she
spread in the proper season, upon the lawn, to
whiten or bleach. Exposed alike with the husband, the wife cheerfully bore with him, the
burden and toil of life. Even sixty years ago,
there could be seen the *Baurbursch*, the youthful
peasant, at the side of him, the *Baurmaedchen*,
the peasant girl, the classic *Puella rustica*, wield-
ing the sickle. Then, this season, *tempus messis*,
harvest time, was one replete with more than

Eleventh. A large strong wagon (*the ship* of inland commerce) covered with linen cloth, is an essential part of the furniture of a German farm. In this wagon drawn by four or five horses of a peculiar breed,* they convey to market, over the roughest roads 2,000 and 3,000 pounds weight of the produce of their farms. In the months of September and October, it is no uncommon thing, on the Lancaster and Reading roads, to meet in one day fifty or one hundred of these wagons, on their way to Philadelphia, most of which belong to German farmers.†

---

ordinary interest to the youthful blood of both sexes, "redolent of joy and youth."

In many parts of Germany, even at this day, the farmer's wives perform field labor, as well as the men. I. D. R.

* The *peculiar breed*, was the *Conestoga horse*, of wide celebrity. The name Conestoga, is from the name of a stream in Lancaster county, along which Swiss Mennonites settled, as early as 1709, '17. They were principally farmers. When the Mennonites first settled in Conestoga valley, the counties of Philadelphia and Chester, had been settled by English emigrants, who brought some horses with them. From this stock, the Conestoga horse was derived. *His. Lan. Co Pa.* pp. 74, &c. *Rep. Com. of Agri.* 1863, pp. 175, 180. I. D. R.

† In 1789, there were no turnpike roads in

NOTE. Some of the first German farmers had
no waggons, no roads to travel upon for a long
time. Some of them occasionally made a waggon
for-using it about the lot; the wheels of those
waggons were made of solid pieces of wood, sawed
round. The harness of the horses were either
ropes or strips of raw hide. I. D. R.

Schoepf, in speaking of the Market in Philadelphia. 1782, says : " Die entfernsten, besonders
deutschen Landleute, kommen mit grossen, mit
mancherlei Proviant beladenen bedeckten Waegen'
auf denen sie zugleich ihren eigenen Mundvorrath
und Futter fuer ihre Pferde mit bringen, und
darauf uebernachten. p. 165 i. e. The most dis-
ant, especially German country people come to
the city, with large covered wagons, laden with
all sorts of provisions; bringing with them, at
the same time, their own victuals, and feed for
their horses, while remaining here.

Pennsylvania. June 21, 1792, the Philadelphia
and Lancaster Turnpike Co. was chartered, which
made and established the first turnpike road laid
in Pennsylvania. It was commenced 1792. finished 1794. It was sixty-two miles in length,
and cost $ 7,500 per mile. The Germantown and
Perkiomen turnpike road was begun 1801, finished 1804, 25 miles in length, cost $ 11, 287
per mile. I. D. R.

Twelfth. The favorable influence of agriculture, as conducted by the Germans, in extending
human happiness, is manifested by the joy, they
express upon the birth of a child.* No dread of
poverty, nor distrust of Providence, from an increasing family, depresses the spirits of these
industrious and frugal people. Upon the birth
of a son, they exult in the gift of a ploughman
or a waggoner; and upon the birth of a daughter,
they rejoice in the addition of another spinster
or milk maid to the family. Happy state of
human society! what blessings can civilization
confer, that can atone for the extinction of the
ancient and patriarchal pleasure of raising up a
numerous and healthy family of children, to labour for their parents, for themselves and for
their country; and finally to partake of the
knowledge and happiness which are annexed to
existence! The joy of parents, upon the birth of
a child, is the greatful echo of creating goodness.
May the mountains of Pennsylvania be forever

---

* Dr. Franklin spake the truth, fully, in saying:
"Agriculture is the only honest way, wherein a
man receives a real increase of seed, thrown into
the ground, in a kind of continued miracle,
wrought by the hand of God, in his favor, for
his innocent life and virtuous industry."   I. D. R.

vocal, with songs of joy, upon these occasions! They will be the infalible signs of innocence, industry, wealth and happiness in the State.

Thirteenth. The Germans take great pains to produce, in their children, not only *habits* of labour, but a *love* of it. In this they submit to the irreversible sentence inflicted upon man, in such a manner as to convert the wrath of heaven into a private and public happiness: "*To fear God, and to love work,*" are the first lessons they teach their children.* They prefer industrious habits to money itself; when a young man asks the consent of his *father* to marry the girl of his choice, *he* does not so much enquire whether she be rich or poor? or whether she possesses any personal or mental accomplishments--

---

* The Germans believed: "Muesiggang, ist des Teufels Ruhebank:" "An idle brain is the devil's workshop." To their children, they said:

Arbeite treu, und glaub es fest
Dass Faulheit aerger ist als Pest,
Der Muesiggang viel Boeses lehrt,
Und alle Art von Suenden mehrt.

Work faithfully: believe 'tis true,
Idleness is worse than a pest;
It is sure, much harm to do,
The cause of gross sins, 'tis confest.

as whether she be industrious, and acquainted
with the duties of a good house-wife-*

Fourteenth. The Germans set a great value
upon patrimonial property. This useful principle
in human nature, prevents much folly and vice in
young people. It moreover leads to lasting and
extensive advantages, in the improvement of a
farm; for what inducement can be stronger in a
parent to plant an orchard† to preserve forest-

---

* The Germans have maxims, which if ob-
served, reduced to practices, will prove advan-
tageous :

Eine fleissige Hausfrau ist die beste Sparbue-
chse—An industrious house-wife is the best
money-safe.

> Erwerben, und sparen zugleich
> Macht am gewissesten reich—
> He that earns and *Saves* will be,
> Rich for certain, you shall see.

In some instances, where the father was not in
favor of the son's or daughter's intended matrimonial alliance, he would cite this proverbial
stanza :

> Der Ehe stand ist ein Huehner haus
> Der eine will hinein. der andre will heraus,
> The marriage state is like a coop, built stout,
> The *outs* would fain be in, the *ins* be out.

† The German axiom reads :

> Im kleinsten Raum pflanz einen Baum
> Und pflege sein, er bringt dir's ein—
> In smallest space, a fruit tree place,
> Attend it well, have fruit to sell.

trees or to build a commodious and durable house, than the idea, that they will all be possessed by a succession of generations, who shall inherit his blood and name.

Fifteenth. The German farmers are very much influenced in planting and pruning trees, also in sowing and reaping, by the age and appearance of the moon. This attention to the state of the moon, has been ascribed to *superstition*,* but if

---

* Call this superstition, or anything else, the German farmers of Pennsylvania, were no more superstitious than others. The common people of England, believe that the moon does exercise great influence on human affairs. The times for killing animals for food, cutting down wood for fuel or other purposes, sowing seeds of various kinds, are all regulated by the age of the moon. *Chamber's Ency. Article, Moon.*

A difference of opinion has ever been entertained by scientific men, as to the moon's influence on the weather, crops, &c, Some maintain that the moon effects the weather, crops, cutting of timber, building of fences, shingling houses. The forest laws of France, interdict the cutting of timber, during the increase of the moon. In the extensive forest of Germany, it is maintained, that wood not felled at the full moon, is very soon attacked by worms and soon rots. The ancient Germans, says *Tacitus*. Coeunt nisi quid fortuitum et subitum incideret, certis diebus, cum aut inchoatur luna, aut impletur nam agendis rebus hoc auspicatissimum initium credunt—*Freely*

the facts related by Mr. Wilson, in his observations upon climates are true, part of their success must be ascribed to their being so much influenced by it.

Sixteenth. From the history that has been given of the German agriculture, it will hardly be necessary to add that a German farm may be distinguished from the farms of the other citizens of the State, by the superior size of their barns ; the plain but compact form of their houses, the height of their inclosures ; the extent of their orchards ; the fertility of their fields ; the luxuriance of their meadows, and a general appearance of plenty and neatness in everything that belonged to them.

The *German mechanic* possesses some of the traits of the character that has been drawn of the *German farmer.* His first object, is to become a freeholder ; and hence we find few of them live in rented houses. The highest compliment that can be paid to them, on entering their houses, is to ask them : *" Is this house your*

---

translated : Unless on some sudden emergency, they assemble on fixed days, either at the new or full moon, which they account the most auspicious season for beginning any enterprise. *De Moribus Germa.* §11. I. D. R.

own?" They are industrious, frugal, punctual
and just. Since their settlement in Pennsylvania,
many of them have acquired the knowledge of
the mechanical arts, which are more immediately
necessary and useful in a new country; while
they continue at the same time, to carry on the
arts they imported from Germany, with vigour
and success.

But the genius of the Germans of Pennsylvania, is not confined to *agriculture* and the *mechanical arts.** As merchants, they are candid
and punctual.

The Bank of North America, has witnessed,
from its first institution, their fidelity to all their
pecuniary engagements.

---

* *David Rittenhouse*, the Astronomer, was of
Swiss or German descent, born 1732, died 1796.
Of him, *Thomas Jefferson* has written: " Rittenhouse is second to no Astronomer living; that in
genius he must be the first, because, he is self-
taught. As an Artist, he has exhibited as great
a proof of mechanical genius as the world has
ever produced. He has not, indeed, made a
world, but has by imitation, approached nearer
its Maker, than any man who has ever lived from
the creation to this day." *Jefferson's Notes of
Va.*, p. 90.

Jefferson alludes in this notice, to the *Orrery,*
constructed by Rittenhouse. I. D. R.

Thus far, I have described the *individual* character of several orders of the German citizens of Pennsylvania. I shall now take notice of some of their manners in a collective capacity. All the different sects among them are particularly attentive to the religious education of their children,* and to the establishment and support of the Christian Religion. For this purpose they settle as much as possible, together, and make the erection of a school-house,† and a place of wor-

---

* This is true of the Lutherans, German Reformed, the Moravians, and in part of the German Brethren, German Seventh Day Baptists, and Mennonites ; but not of some sects, who are now defunct. Pennsylvania, was once the *arena*, where Labadists, the society of the Woman in the Wilderness, Zions Brueder, New Born, Rondoerfer, Inspired, Separatists, Quietists, Gichtlians, Dipellians—made a display of " *their subjective piety.*" I. D. R.

† Schools, they considered the most precious jewels of the church. If no school-master was to be had, the minister would attend to the instructions of the youth, in reading, writing, casting accounts. In 1749, there came to Pennsylvania, twelve school-masters with German immigrants. With the Germans, it was a leading concern to have among them, the minister and the school-master ; for they well knew " a people may be destroyed for lack of knowledge." *Hall. Nach.* *pp.* 66 *and* 391. I. D. R.

ship, the first object of their care. They commit the education and instruction of their children, in a peculiar manner, to the ministers and officers of their churches; hence they grow up with *biases* in favor of public worship, and of the obligations of Christianity. Such has been the iufluence of a pious education among the *Germans*, in Pennsylvania, that in the coursc of nineteen years, only *one* of them, has ever been brought to a place of public shame or punishment—(*Worthy of note*).

As members of civil government, the Germans are peaceable,* and exact in the payment of their taxes.† Since they have participated in

---

* A late writer bears the Germans this testimony: "Whether a denizen of a state be valuable to it on account of what he annually adds to the realized wealth of the community, or for his faithful obedience to the laws or for the sacredness with which he preserves the family compact, our *German farmers* certainly merit as much as any other class for the practice of either of these virtues, or indeed for the harmonious exercise of all."—*Phila. Ledger*, 1856. I. D. R.

† It has been well said : "One of our richest men invariably spreads his *papers* before the Assessor, and tells him to tax him, according to his mind. A genuine Pennsylvania German buys

the power of the state, many of them have become sensible and enlightened in the science of
legislation. Pennsylvania has had the speaker's
chair of her assembly, and the Vice-president's
office of her council, filled with dignity, by gen-
tlemen of German families. The same gentle-
men have since been advanced to seats in the
House of Representatives, under the new constitution of the United States. In the great con-
troversy about the national government, a large
majority of the Germans in Pennsylvania, decided
in favor of its adoption, notwithstanding the
most popular arts were used to prejudice them
against it.*

---

for cash; or never, unless he sees the avenue by
which the means are to flow into his hands. Our
wives don't own their husband's property. Ped-
lers and venders lose less among us, than by other
folks. *C. Z. W. Ref. Church Messenger*, 1868,
I. D. R.

* May 15, 1775, a *Committee of Observation*
for the borough and county of Lancaster, was
held at the house of Adam Reigart, on which
occasion measures were adopted to hold elections
in the several townships of Lancaster county, to
choose committees of vigilance. Among the
number chosen of these committees. many were
Germans, viz. Bausman, Klatz, Voght, Dehuff,
Krug, Musser, Reigert Schaffner, Slauch, Graff,

The Germans are but little addicted to convivial pleasures. They seldom meet for the simple purpose of eating and drinking, in what are justly called: "*Feeding parties,*" but they are no strangers to the virtue of hospitality.*

Brubacher, Huber, Bachman, Rathvon, Rupley, Funk, Haberstick, Neucomer, Lefever, Gruber, Brechbill, Wittman, Kendig, Greiner, Erb, Kratzer, Heil, Stehley, Royer, Grill, Flick, Rein, Roland, Weber, Guth, Bobb, Eckert, Ley, De-Haas, Gruenewalt, Licht, Kohr, Beshore, Lang, Haldeman.

July 4, 1776, a meeting was held at Lancaster, consisting of the officers and privates of fifty-three battalions of the Associators of the Colony of Pennsylvania, to choose two Brigadier Generals. Several counties were represented by Germans, viz: from *Bucks,* by Herr, Steinbach, Mittelsworth, Titus. From *Lancaster co.,* Slauch, Ferrie, Reigert, Rathvon, Weiman, Marsthaler, Scherer, Weber, Wirtz, Zearing, Derr, Schleiermacker, Buch, Schneider, Lein, Diffenbach, Doebler. From *York co.,* Diehl, Kraft, Schmeiser, Schlei. From *Berks co.,* Levan, Hiester, Lindemuth, Loeffler, Kremer, Lutz, Mueller, Ebe, Keim, May, Hartmann, Filbert, Spohn, Wenrich, Moser, Seltzer, Wuester, Schmack. From *Northampton co.,* Geiger, Leber, Siegfried, Orndt, Schneider, Kern, Opp, Berghaus, Braun, Best, Von Fleck. *Rupp's His. Lan. co.* pp. 396-406.

* Tacitus, a Latin Historian, born A. D., 56, died 135, in his *De Moribus Germaniae,* bears

[Germans of Pennsylvania, give heed to the precept in the moral code of their adoption: Gastfrey zuseyn vergesset nicht. Heb; 13; 2 1. D. R.] The hungry or benighted traveller, is always sure to find a hearty welcome under their roofs. A gentleman of Irish extraction, who lost his way in travelling through Lancaster county, called late at night at the door of a German farmer. He was kindly received and entertained with the best of everything the house afforded. The next morning, he offered to pay his host for his lodg-

---

the ancient Germans this testimony: Convictibus et hospitiis non alia gens effusius indulget. Quemcumque mortalium arcere tecto, nefas habetur: profortuna quisque adparatis epulis excipit. Comdefecere, qui modo hospes fuerat, monstrator hospitii et comes, proximam domum not invitati ad euntnec interest: pari humanitate accipiuntur. Notum ignotumpue, quantum ad jus hospitii, nemo discernit. *Freely translated:* Hospitality and convivial pleasures are no where so liberally enjoyed. To refuse admittance to any person were an outrage against humanity. The master of the house welcomes every stranger, and regales him to the best of his ability. When his provisions are exhausted, he goes to his neighbor, conducts his new acquaintance to another hospitable board. They do not wait to be invited; are received mast cordially. Between an intimate friend and a stranger no distinction is made. I. D. R,

ing, and other accommodations : " *No,*" said the friendly German, in broken English—" I will take nothing from you, I was once lost, and entertained, as you have been at the house of a stranger, who would take no pay from me for his trouble. I am, therefore, now only discharging that debt.—do you pay your debt to me in the same way, to somebody else."*

They are extremely kind and friendly as neighbors. They often assist each other by loans of money for a short time, when the purchase of a plantation makes a larger sum necessary, than is commonly possessed by a single farmer. To secure their confidence, it is necessary to be punctual.† They never lend money a *second* time, to a man who has *once* disappointed them in paying what he borrowed agreeably to his promise or obligation. It was remarked, during the late war, that there were very few instances of any of

---

* The most liberal hospitality and disinterestedness, mark the character of the Germans in Europe. *Goldsmith's Manners and Customs of Nations*, pa. 64.

† Wer puenctlich bezahlt, mag wieder borgen. He that pays punctually can borrow again. *Koerte's Sprichwoerter.* I. D. R.

them discharging a bond, or a debt, with depreciated paper money.

It has been said, that the Germans are deficient
in learning,* and in consequence of their want of
more general and extensive education, they are

---

* This charge, against the Germans of Pennsylvania, is a *stale* one, though still reiterated.
The Germans says, C. Z. W. are not opposed to
education. They are proud of a cultivated ministry, treat all with proverbial respect. *They* of
all others, usually, took good care to build a
school-house near the church. They of all others,
speak of the *"School-Master,"* as next to the
pastor. Of a training *in Christ* they stand
behind none, of *a certain kind* of education.
But *" Free Schools,"* in the sense of divorcing
them from the church, they never yet have
learned heartly to love. And as long as a rem-
nant of the former healthy echo remains, we
affirm, they never will. Hence, too, they are
slow in sending their sons and daughters abroad.
They believe that much of the *" Stuff "* that is
administered to their offspring in such quarters,
renders them *proud, lazy* and *infidel.* And now,
after you are done laughing and *poohing* at such
a silly notion of those foolish Pennsylvania Germans, just please, ask yourself soberly and
conscientiously, whether there is not something in
it after all"—(*Ref, Mess.* 1868.) The Germans are
not all *Vetter Michels, Cousin Michaels* in ap-
proving of what is useful. *Cui bono ?* Is a
question with them. I. D. R.

much addicted to superstition, and are frequeutly imposed upon in the management of their affairs. Many of them have lost valuable estates, by being unacquainted with the common forms of law, in the most simple transactions; many more of them have lost their lives, by applying to *quacks*,* in sickness : but this objection to the Germans, will soon cease to have any foundation in Pennsylvania. Several young men, born of German parents, have been educated in law, physic and divinity, who have demonstrated by their abilities and knowledge, that the German genius, for literature has not depreciated in America.

[NOTE. There lived at Hilspach, not far from Neckar Gemuend, near Heidelberg, *Johannes Caspar Wuester*—two of his sons emigrated to Pennsylvania, Caspar, in 1717, and Johannes, in 1727. Of the grandson of *Caspar*, Davenport

---

* There is no doubt of the fact, that some lost their lives by applying to *Quacks*. Are there not *diplomated quacks*, created such by sheepskins, written in Latin, which few of the holders can read and translate. The country swarms with thrasonical sciolist in the *"healing art."* I. D. R.

says : " *Caspar Wistar*, a celebrated physician, was born in Philadelphia, in 1761. He studied medicine under Dr. John Redman, and completed his professional course at the schools in London and Edinburg. Returning in 1787, to his native city, he soon distinguished himself in his profession, and in 1789, was elected professor of chemistry, in the college of Philadelphia. In 1792, he became adjunct professor of anatomy, midwifery, and surgery, with Dr. Shippen ; and, on the decease of that gentleman, in 1808, sole professor. His acquirements in professional knowledge were very extensive, and he obtained much popularity as a lecturer   His chief work is a valuable system of *Anatomy, in two volumes.* He died 1819." I. D. R.]

A college has lately been founded by the state, in Lancaster,† and committed chiefly to the care

---

† March 10th, 1787, the General Assembly of Pennsylvania, passed an Act, entitled: " An Act to incorporate and endow the German College, Charity School, in the borough of Lancaster. The Preamble explains the object, intended : " Whereas, the citizens of this state, of German birth or extraction, have eminently contributed, by their industry, economy and public virtues, to raise the state to its present happiness and pros-

of the Germans of all sects, for the purpose of
diffusing learning among their children. [The
College was called Franklin, after *Dr. Benjamin
Franklin*, who contributed largely to its funds.
I. D. R.]. In this college they are to be taught
the German and English languages, and all those
branches of literature which are usually taught
in the colleges of Europe and America, The
principal of this college is a native of Pennsyl-

---

perity; and, whereas, a number of citizens of
the above description, in conjunction with others,
from a desire to increase and perpetuate the blessings derived to them from the possession of property and a free government, have applied to this
House for a charter of incorporation, &c. and
whereas, the preservation of the principles of the
Christian Religion, and of our Republican form
of Government in their purity, depend under
God, in a great measure on the establishment and
support of suitable places of education, for the
purpose of training a succession of youth, who,
by being enabled fully to understand the grounds
of both, may be led the more zealously to practice the one, and the more strenously to defend the
other." * * * * That the youth shall be
taught in German, English, Latin, Greek and
other learned Languages, in Theology, in the
useful arts, sciences and literature." It is now
known by the name of *Franklin and Marshall,*
and is under the tutelary care of the German
Reformed church. I. D. R.

vania, of German parentage.* His extensive
knowledge and taste in the arts and sciences,
joined with his industry in the discharge of the
duties of his station, have afforded to the friends
of learning in Pennsylvania, the most flattering
prospects of the future importance and usefulness
of this institution.

Both sexes of the Germans discover a strong
propensity to vocal and instrumental music.
They excell, in *Psalmody all the other religious*
societies in the State.† The freedom and tolera-

---

* *Rev. Henry Ernest Muhlenberg, D. D.*, (son
of Henry Melchior Muhlenberg, D. D.)—he was
born in Montgomery county, Pa., Nov. 17, 1753.
At the age of ten years, he was sent to Halle,
Germany, with his two elder brothers, to finish
his education. On his return to Pa., 1770, he
was ordained, at the early age of seventeen;—in
1774, appointed assistant to his father, in the
Philadelphia congregation. In 1780, he accepted
a call from the Lutheran church, in Lancaster,
where he resided thirty-five years. He died,
May 23, 1815. I. D. R.

† In all the parochial schools of Lutheran
and German Reformed church, vocal music was
taught. At Ephrata, Lancaster Co., vocal music was much cultivated. Conrad Beissel, the
Founder of the *Sieben Taeger Society*, was a first
rate musician and composer. "The counter,
treble tenor and bass were all sung by women,

tion of the government have produced a variety of sects among the Germans in Pennsylvania. The Lutherans compose a great portion of the German citizens of the State. The German Presbyterians, (Reformed) are the next in number. Their churches are likewise large, and furnished in many places, with organs. The clergy belonging to these churches, have moderate salaries; but they are punctually and justly paid. In the country they have *glebes* which are stocked, and occasionally worked by their congregation. By this means the discipline and the general interests of their churches are preserved. The Lutherans and Presbyterians,* (German Reformed), live in great harmony with each other, insomuch that they preach in each other's churches, and in some instances, *unite* in building a church, in

---

with sweet, shrill and small voices, but with a truthful, exactness in time, and intonation, that was admirable. *See History of Lancaster Co.*, pp. 226, &c.. I. D. R.

* *Presbyterians*—this is a *misnomer*—it should be German Reformed—various misnomers have been applied, by certain writers, to the German Reformed church. Gordon, in his history of New Jersey, calls them: " *The German Reformed Lutheran Church.*" I. D. R.

which they both worship at different times. This harmony between the two sects, one so much opposed to each other, is owing to the relaxation of the Presbyterians, (Ger. Ref.) in some of the peculiar doctrines of Calvinism.*

The Mennonites, the Moravians, the Schwenk-felders, Catholics, [and Omish, or Amish, a German sect. I. D. R.] compose the other sects of the German inhabitants of Pennsylvania. The Mennonites hold war and oaths to be unlawful. They administer the sacrements of baptism by *sprinkling*,† and observe the supper. From them a *sect* has arisen, who hold with the above principals and ceremonies, the necessity of immersion baptism, hence they are called *Dunkers*,

---

* The *Heidelberg Catechism*, the symbolical book adopted by the German Reformed church, is, in its general character, Calvinistic. This formulary observes a singular moderation on some points, upon which the several parties in the Protestant churches differed, or respecting which good men might entertain different opinions. The Heidelberg Catechism is more *irenical* than otherwise. I. D. R.

† The Mennonites baptize the subject while kneeling, by *pouring* water upon the head of the person being baptized. I. D. R.

or Baptists.* Previously to their partaking, of
the sacrement of the supper, they wash each
other's feet, and sit down to a love-feast. They
practice these ceremonies of their religion, with
great humility and solemnity. They, moreover
hold the doctrine of universal salvation. [This
last clause must be received *cum grano salis.*
I. D. R.] From this sect, there have been
several seceders, one of whom devoted themselves to perpetual celibacy.† They have exhibited

---

* *Dr. Rush's* statement lacks historical proof.
The *Dunkers* (German Brethren), as a sect, have
not arisen from the Mennonites. Alexander
Mack, of Vitchengestein, of Prussia, founded,
1708, this sect, Rev. Peter Becker, one of the
German Brethren ministers came to Pennsylvania, 1719. Alexander Mack followed Becker to
Pennsylvania, 1729, settled near Germantown—
died 1735, aged 65—buried in Brethren burying-
ground, at Germantown. I. D. R.

† *Conrad Peysel,* or *Beissel,* born 1691, at
Oberbach in the Palatinate. He was educated for
the gospel ministry, at Halle, once the principal
seat of Pietistic divines of Germany. Beissel,
by reason of his peculiar opinions on some points
of Theology was coolly treated by the confrater-
nity. He left Halle, went to Friesland, Holland,
resided for sometime at Serustervin, formed the
acquaintance of disciples of Alexander Mack.
Ency. Rel. Knowledge, 479.

for many years, a curious spectacle of pious mortification, at a village called Ephrata, Lancaster County : They are at present, 1787, reduced to fourteen or fifteen members.

The *Separatists* who likewise dissented from the Dunkers, reject the ordinance of baptism and the sacrament of *the supper*; and hold the doctrine of the *Friends*, concerning the internal revelation of the gospel. They hold with the Dunkers, the doctrine of universal salvation. The singular piety, and exemplary morality of these sects, has been urged by the advocates for the salvation of all mankind, as a proof that the

---

In 1719, Beissel came to Pennsylvania, with *Peter Beeker*, a leader of the German Brethren—resided for some time at *Muelback*, Lancaster Co. now Lebanon. He published a *Tract*, 1725, showing that the German Brethren were in error, in observing the first day of the week, instead of Saturday. This Tract produced quite an excitement at Muelbach. Beissel seceded, 1728, located at Ephrata, founded *the Sieben Taegar Taeufer* Denomination. He was a man of peculiar *idiosyncracy*. In personal appearance, when sixty-four years of age, it is said : " He was a small lean man, had gray bushy hair, quick in his utterance, as well as in his movements." *Acrelius, p.* 373. Beissel died July 6, 1768, buried at Ephrata.

belief of that doctrine is not unfriendly to morals, and the order of society, as has been supposed. The Dunkers and Separatists agree in taking no interest upon money, and in not applying to law to recover their debts.

The German Moravians are a numerous and respectable body of christians in Pennsylvania. In their village of Bethlehem,* there are two large stone buildings, in which the different sexes are educated in the habits of industry, in useful manufactures. The sisters, (for by that epithet the women are called,) all sleep in two large and neat apartments. Two of them watch over the rest, in turns, every night, to afford relief from those sudden indispositions which sometimes occur, in the most healthy persons, in the hours of sleep. It is impossible to record this fact, without pausing a moment to do homage to that religion, which produced so much union and kindness in human souls. The number of women, who belong to this sequestured female society, amounts sometimes to one hundred and twenty, and seldom to less than one hundred. It is re-

---

* *Bethlehem* : a Moravian settlement commenced here, 1742. I. D. R.

markable that notwithstanding, they lead a sedentary life, and sit constantly in close store-rooms in winter, that not more than one of them, upon an average, dies in a year. The diseases which generally produces their annual death, is the consumption. The conditions and ages of the women of the village, as well as of the society that has been mentioned, are distinguished by ribbons of a peculiar kind which they wear on their caps—the widows, by *blue*, the single women, above eighteen years of age, by *pink;* and those under that age, by a ribbon of a cin-namon colour.

Formerly this body of Moravians held all their property in common in imitation of the primitive christians ; but, in 1760, a division of the whole took place, except a tavern and a tanyard, 2,000 acres of land near Bethlehem, and 5,000 acres near Nazareth, a village in the neighborhood of Bethlehem. The profits of these estates are ap-propriated to the support and propagation of the gospel. There are many valuable manufactures carried on at Bethlehem. The inhabitants possess a gentleness in their manners, which is peculiarly agreeable to strangers. They inure their chil-dren, of five and six years old, to habits of early industry. By this means they are not only taught those kinds of labor which are suited to their strength and capacities, but are preserved from many of the hurtful vices and accidents to which children are exposed.

The Schwenkfelders are a small society. They hold the same principles as the Friends, but they differ from them in using psalmody in their worship.* The German Catholics are numerous in Philadelphia, and have small chapels in other parts of the state.†

There is an incorporated charitable society of

---

*This denomination of christians, is so called after *Casper Schwenkfeld* von Ossing, a Silesian knight. He was born 1490. In 1734, some of the Schwenkfelders came to Pennsylvania, settled principally in Montgomery, Berks, Bucks and Lehigh Counties, Pa. Dr. Rush does not specify when he says: "*they hold the same principles as the Friends.*" The Schwenkfelders do not reject the sacraments, baptism and the Lord's Supper. They maintain that Christ commanded his disciples to baptize with water, and to observe the Lord's Supper. *See. Rev. Christopher Schultz' Catechism*, ppa. 80-92, translated, *by me, and published at Skippackville, Pa.*, 1863. I. D. R.

† Because the *Germans* would not dance when Political demagogues piped when *they* numbered above 200.000, in 1754, it was alleged by way of a stigma upon their character, that one fourth of the Germans were Roman Catholics! One

Germans, in Philadelphia, whose objects are their poor and distressed countrymen.*

___

fourth of 200.000, would be 50.000. All the Roman Catholics, including English, Irish and German, men, women and children, did not num- 2.000, in 1757. *List of German Catholics, 1757,* of all such as received the sacraments from 12 years of age and upwards, viz:—Under the care of *Theodore Schneider,* in and about Philadelphia, 107 males, 121 females; in Philadelphia co., up the country, 75 males, 10 females; in Berks Co., 62 males, 55 females; in Northampton Co., 68 males, 62 females; Bucks Co., 14 males, 12 fe- males; Chester Co., 13 males, 9 females, Under the care of *Ferdinand Farmer,* in Lancaster Co., 108 males, 94 females; in Berks Co., 41 males, 39 females; in Chester Co., 3 males. Under the care of *Mathias Manners,* in York Co., (inclu- ding Adams,) 54 males and 62 females, total 949. The Irish Catholics in Pennsylvania, numbered only 418. Under the care of *Robert Harding,* in and about Philadelphia, 72 males, 78 females,; in Chester Co., 18 males, 22 females. Under the care of *Theodore Schneider,* in Northampton Co. 17 males, 12 females; in Chester Co., 9 males, 6 females. Under the care of *Ferdinand Far- mer;* in Lancaster Co., 22 males, 27 females; Berks Co., 5 males, 3 females; in Chester Co., 23 males, 17 females; in Cumberland Co., 9 males, 9 females. Under the care of *Mathias Manners;* in York Co., (including Adams,) 35 males, 38 fe- males. *Col. Rec.* VII, 447. *Penna, Archives,* III. 144, 145. *See Fireside History of German and Swiss Immigrants.*

* The German Society of Philadelphia, in the

There is likewise, a German Society of labourers and journeymen mechanics, who contributed 2s. 6d. eight times a year towards a fund, out

Province of Pennsylvania, was incorporated, 1764. This Society supplied the poor, the sick and otherwise distressed Germans * * * to teach and improve their poor children, both in English and German Languages, reading and writing thereof, and to procure for them such learning and education, as would best suit their genius and capacities, and enable the proper objects to receive the finishing of their studies in the University of Philadelphia; likewise to erect a Library, &c. The Library 1875, contains some twenty thousand volumes.

The officers of the Society, named in the act of incorporation were—Henry Keppele, *Pres.* Lewis Weiss. V. P. ; Lewis Farmer and Henry Leuthaeuser, *Sect'y;* Christoph Ludwig, Peter Ozeas, Andrew Burkhard, John Fritz. Peter Kraft and Melchior Steiner, *Overseers;* Michael Schubart, *Treas.;* Henry Kaemmerer, *Solicitor;* William Lehman, Deacon. I. D. R.

Soon after the organization of the German Society, in Philadelphia, a similar one was formed in Baltimore. The *German Friendly Society* of Charleston, S. C., was organized 1766, by *Michael Kalteisen,* Melchior Warley, Johann Schwint, Abraham Speidel, Johann Lehre, Christian Dus, Carl Gruber, Philip Mintzing, Martin Miller, Jacob Breigel, Daniel Strobel, Conrad Burkmeyer, Friedrich Hoff, Eberhard Ehney, Johann Kelle and Frederick Mattutz. *Der Deutsche Pionier,* III, 7. I. D. R.

of which they allow 30s. a week to each other's families, when the head of it is unable to work; and £ 7, 10s. to his widow, as soon as he is taken from his family by death.

The Germans of Pennsylvania, including all the sects that have been mentioned, compose nearly *one third part* of the whole inhabitants of the State.*

The intercourse of the Germans with each other, is kept up chiefly in their own language; but most of their men who visit the capital, and trading or country towns of the state, speak the

---

* The total population, in round numbers, was then 435.000, one third Germans, which is 145.000. *Ebeling says:* that in 1790 the German population of Pennsylvania, was 144.660, *Ebeling*, p. 202. According to the *Census* of 1870. the aggregate population was 3.521.795, of this number, who were born in Germany, was 160.146. The German born and the descendants of Germans, are not less than 1.200.000. Within the last forty years upwards of 2.000.000, of Germans immigrated to the United States. The German element is not as insignificant as some would suppose it to be. A learned Professor, has called the collective, Germans of Pennsylvania: "*A giant asleep.*" Fitting appliances may arouse the "*giant.*" The total German population, on the inhabitable globe is about 65.000.000. I. D. R.

English language. A certain number of the laws are now printed in German, for the benefit of those of them, who cannot read English. A large number of German news-papers are likewise circulated through the State, through which knowledge and intelligence have been conveyed, much to the advantage of the government. There is scarcely an instance of a German, of either sex, in Pennsylvania, that cannot *read ;* but many of the wives and daughters of the German farmers cannot *write.* The present state of society among them renders this accomplishment of little consequence to their improvement or happiness.

If it were possible, to determine the amount of all the property brought into Pennsylvania, by the present German inhabitants of the state, and their ancestors, and then compare it with the present amount of their property, the contrast would form such a monument of *human industry and economy,* as has seldom been contemplated in any age or country.

I have been informed that there was an ancient prophecy which foretold, that " *God would bless the Germans in foreign countries.*" This prediction has been faithfully verified in Pennsylvania. They enjoy here every blessing that liberty, toleration, independence, affluence, virtue and reputation, can confer upon them.

How different is their situation here, from what it was in Germany. Could the subjects of the prince of Germany, who now groan away their lives in slavery and unprofitable labour, view from an eminence, in the month of June, the German settlements of Strasburg or Manheim, in Lancaster county, or of Lebanon, in Dauphin county, or Bethlehem in Northampton county— could they be accompanied on this eminence, by a venerable German farmer, and be told by him that many of those extensive fields of grain, full fed herds, luxuriant meadows, orchards, promising loads of fruit, together with the spacious barns— and commodious stone-dwelling houses, which compose prospects that have been mentioned, were all the product of the labour of a single family, and of *one* generation; and they were all secured to the owners of them by *certain laws;* I am persuaded, that no chains would be able to detain them from sharing in the freedom of their Pennsylvania friends and former fellow subjects. " *We will assert our dignity* (would be their language)— *Will be men—we will be free—we will* *enjoy the fruits of our onn labour—we will no longer be bought and sold to fight battles*—in which we have neither interest nor resentment—we will inherit a portion of that blessing which God has promised to the Germans in foreign countries— we will be Pennsylvanians."*

I shall conclude this *Account* of the Manners of the German inhabitants of Pennsylvania, by remarking that if I have failed in doing them

---

* Germans had been sold by their *Lords*, to England, to fight battles in which they had no interest, at several periods—1702, 1726, 1743, 1745. In the *prosopopaeia : "we will no longer be bought and sold,"* are personated collectively Germans, called *Huelfs truppen,* subsidiary-troops, sold by several German Dukes, Landgraves, Margraves to the king of England, 1776-1783, to wage an exterminating war against the American Colonies. The Duke of Brunswick sold 5,733; the Prince of Hanau, 2,422; the Margrave of Anspach, 1,644; the Prince of Waldeck, 1,225; the Prince of Anhalt Zerbst, 1,160; the Landgrave of Hesse Cassel, 1,200; the Hereditary Prince of Hesse Cassel 796; the Margrave of Brandenberg, 1,200—Besides others. The aggregate number of these Germans that *perished in battle,* exceeded upwards of *eleven thousand.*

The sale of these subjects was a profitable business to their *humane lords.* The sum total paid by His Britanic Majesty to the several Princes, Dukes, was $8,100,000. I. D. R.

justice, it has not been the *fault* of my subject.
The *German character* once employed the pen
of one of the first Historians of antiquity. I
mean the elegant and enlightened *Tacitus*. It
is very remarkable that the Germans in Pennsylvania, retain in a great degree, all the virtues
which *Tacitus* ascribes to their ancestors in his
treaties *De Moribus Germanorum*. They inherit
their *integrity—fidelity and chastity*,* but chris-
itanity has banished from them, their drunkeness,
idleness and love of military glory. There is a singular trait in the features of the German character in Pennsylvania, which shows how long the
most trifling custom may exist among a people who
have not been mixed with other nations.

---

* Severa illic matrimonia: nec ullam morem
partem magis laudaveris: The matrimonial bond
is strict and severe among them; nor is there
anything in their manners more commendable
than this. I. D. R.

Some *refined* ladies, mothers of infants, might
safely follow German mothers in Pennsylvania, or
the ancient German mothers: Sua quemque ma-
ter uberibus alit, nec ancillis ac nutricibus delega-
ntur: i. e. Every mother suckles her own children, and does not deliver them into the hands of
servants and nurses. *Dac. De. Mor. Ger.* § 18
and 20.

Tacitus describes in the following words, in which the ancient Germans built their villages : "Suam quisque domum circumdat sive adversus casus ignis remedium, sive inscitia aedificandi." (each man leaves a space between his house, and those of his neighbors, either to avoid the danger from fire, or from unskillfulness in architecture).

Many of the German villages in Pennsylvania, are constructed in the same manner. The small houses are composed of a mixture, of wood, brick and clay, neatly united. The large houses are built of stone, and many of them after the English fashion. Very few of the houses in Germantown, are connected together. Where the Germans connect their houses in their villages, they appear to have deviated from one of the customs they imported from Germany.

Citizens of the United States learn from the account given of the German Inhabitants of Pennsylvania, to prize knowledge and industry in *agriculture* and manufactures, as the basis of domestic happiness and national prosperity.*

* It has been well said by *Sully,* (born 1559, died 1641), "*agriculture* may be regarded as the breasts from which the State derives its support and nourishment." I. D. R.

Legislatures of the United States, learn from
the wealth, and independence of the German
inhabitants of Pennsylvania, to encourage by
your example, and laws, the republican virtues
of industry and economy. They are the only
pillars which can support the present constitution
of the United States.*

Legislators of Pennsylvania, learn from the
history of your German fellow citizens, that you
possess an inexhaustible treasure in the bosom
of the State, in their manners and arts. Continue to patronize their newly established Semi-
nary, (Franklin College), of learning, and spare
no expense in supporting their free-schools. The
vices which follow the want of religious instructions, among the children of poor people, lay the
foundations of most of the jails and places of
public punishment in the State. Do not contend
with their prejudices in favor of their language.†

---

* It was to the German *Bauern*, Farmers,
America owed her independence. They were
among the first to shoulder the gun, they were
the bravest and most enduring of Washington's
soldiers. *Peasant Life in Germany*, 389.
I. D. R.

† In 1729, ambitious, disappointed politicians
were opposed to Germans. It was an objection to

It will be the channel through which the knowledge and discoveries of the wisest nations in Europe, may be conveyed into our country. In proportion as they are instructed and enlightened in their *own language*, they will become acquainted with the language of the United States. Invite them to share in the power and offices of government: it will be the means of producing an union in principle and conduct between them, and those of their enlightened fellow-citizens, who are descended from other nations, Above all, cherish with peculiar tenderness, those sects among them who hold war to be unlawful.* Relieve them from the oppression of absurd and

---

the *wise-acres* of the times, because "the Germans adhered to each other, and that they used *exclusively* the German language." (Gordon's Pa., 107). The same sort of politicians, because they had failed to succeed in getting the Germans to vote for them, seriously proposed, 1754: "that the government should suspend the right of the *Germans* to vote for the members of the Assembly, until they had acquired a competent knowledge of the *English Language*." *Watson's Annals*, II. 275. I. D. R.

* Rush alludes to the Mennonites, German Brethren, Moravians, German Seventh Day Baptists and Schwenkfelders, who hold war to be *unchristian* and *unreasonable*. I D. R.

unnecessary militia laws. Protect them as the repositories of the truth of the gospel, which has existed in every age of the church, and which must spread over every part of the world.

The opinions respecting the commerce and slavery of the Africans, which have nearly produced a revolution in their favour, in some of the European governments, were transplanted from a sect of Christians in Pennsylvania.* Perhaps those German sects of christians among us, who refuse to bear arms for the purpose of shedding human blood, may be preserved by divine providence as the centre of a circle, which shall gradually embrace all nations of the earth in a perpetual treaty of friendship and peace. *Finis.*

---

* "It is to the honor of *German Friends* of Germantown, that as early as 1688, they addressed the Philadelphia Yearly Meeting, at Burlington," protesting against buying, selling and holding men in slavery, and declaring it, in their opinion, an act irreconcilable with the precepts of the christian religion. *Watson's Annals*, II, 23. I. D. R.

NOTE TO PAGE 60.

Benjamin Franklin, otherwise an astute States-
man and a Philosopher, with his Yankee prejudices, coincided with the *wise-acres* of the times.
In a letter to *Peter Collinson*, May 9, 1753, he
writes : "I am perfectly of your mind, that measures of great temper are necessary touching the
Germans, and am not without apprehensions, that,
through their indiscretion, or ours, or both, great
disorders may one day arise among us. Those
who come hither are generally the most stupid of
their own nation, and as ignorance is often at-
tended with great credulity, when knavery would
mislead it, and with suspicion when honesty would
set it right; and, few of the English understand
the German language, and so cannot address them
either from the press or pulpit, it is almost impossible to remove any prejudices they may
entertain. Their clergy have very little influence
on the people, who seem to take pleasure in
abusing and discharging the minister on every
trivial occasion, Not being used to liberty, they
know not how to make modest use of it, * * *
They are under no restraint from ecclesiastical
government; they behave, however, submissively
enough at present to the civil government, which
I wish they may continue to do, for I remember
when they modestly declined intermeddling with

our elections ; but now they come in droves and carry all before them, except in one or two counties.

Few of their children in the country know English. They import many books from Germany, and, of the six printing-houses in the province, two are entirely German, two half German, half English, and but two are entirely English. They have one German newspaper, and one half German. Advertisements intended to be general, are now printed in Dutch, (German) and English. The signs in our streets, (Philada.) have inscriptions in both languages, and some places only in German. They begin, of late, to make all their bonds and other legal instruments in their own language, which (though I think it ought not to be), are allowed good in our courts, where the German business so increases, that there is continued need of interpreters, and I suppose in a few years, they will also be necessary in the Assembly, to tell one half of our legislators, what the other half says. In short, unless the stream of importation could be turned from this to other colonies, as you very judiciously propose, they will soon so outnumber us, that all the advantages we have, will, in my opinion, be not able to preserve our language, and even our government will become precarious." *Sparks'* *Works of Franklin VII, pp.* 71,-73.

APPENDIX.

The German Farmers of Pennsylvania, have once and again been maliciously aspersed by partisan Editors of "*pliant sheets.*" The Germans of Pennsylvania, have been too long left at the mercy of misrepresentation and detraction of base calumniators, *Verleumders.*

The *Editor* of the *Public Ledger,* who is familiar with his German fellow citizens, justly vindicates them, in his strictures on an article, which appeared in a newspaper, published 1856:

"A Buffalo newspaper, in a late article on the *German Farmers of Pennsylvania* informs the world that they are hardly more intelligent or independent than the serfs of the Fatherland a century and a half ago, "The immigrants came over here with their Priests" it says: "a fragment of the middle ages, uneducated and uncultivated. What is the consequence? We see before us the petrification of a social and mental condition which has long since disappeared from Germany. We behold a picture of the dark and gloomy middle ages."

Remarks by the Editor of the Public Ledger.

" No one familiar with the *German farmers of Pennsylvania,* need be told that this is a stupid and ignorant libel. Its author has either never travelled through our State, or has maliciously misrepresented what he saw. So far from our German farmers being on a level with the serfs of a hundred and fifty years ago, they are vastly in advance of contemporary German or French farmers, or even of English farmers of similar means. On this point we need go no further for authority than to Mr. Munch, the fellow laborer with Herder in the late campaign, who though hostile in politics to our German farmers in general, was forced, during his tour through Pennsylvania, to admit their sterling worth. Mr. Munch is an experienced and practical agriculturalist, and not merely a speculative man of letters, so that his judgment on such a question is worth that of a score of visionary, ill-informed, prejudiced, disappointed demagogues or partisan editors. After eulogizing the picturesque natural features of the landscape of our German counties, praising the excellent taste which has preserved the woods on the hill-sides, and extolling the appearance of the farms, this gentleman adds significantly that he found the population of " a genial, solid and respectable stamp, enviably circumstanced in comparison with the European farmer, and very far his superior in intelligence and morals."

"It is time that truth should be spoken, and justice done to our German population. We are willing to go as far as any one in testifying to the value of books, newspapers and schools; we are willing to admit that our German farmers, as a class, have cared less for these things than they ought; but we are not yet silly enough to say that a man is necessarily a bad farmer, a disorderly citizen, or a profligate husband because he does not *speak English*, is not crammed with book-learning, or does not take in half a dozen journals. Our German farmers prove the reverse. Whether a denizen of a State be valuable to it on account of what he annually adds to the realized wealth of the community, or for his faithful obedience to the laws, or for the sacredness with which he preserves the family compact, our German farmers certainly merit as much as any other class for the practice of either of these virtues, or indeed for the harmonious exercise of all. Even their intelligence is popularly underrated. As Mr. Munch, of Misso, has said, they are of a " *genial, solid and respectable stamp :*" there is no false mental glitter about them : in a word, they are rather men of sound judgment, than brilliant rhetoricians or one sided ideologists. All persons who have had transactions with our German farmers, learn to respect the excellent sense they display in the ordinary concerns of life. It is only when po-

litical difference arise, that our Germans are
stigmatized as dolts. Would it not be more con-
sistent, not to say liberal, to give the Germans
credit for equal honesty and shrewdness, in public affairs, as in private? Are those who denounce
the Germans, because of their votes, possessed
of a monopoly of the intelligence and patriotism
of the republic?

But we are willing to waive this part of the
question. There are other things, besides political soundness, valuable in a citizen. In many
particulars, German farmers surpass even the
people of New England, who, of late, have put
in a claim, it would seem to be the *ne plus ultra*
in all things. The *German farmers* understand,
or if they do not understand, they observe the
laws of health, better than even the rural population of Massachusetts; and the result is that
they are really the finest race of men, physically,
to be found within the borders of the United
States. In certain favorable localities of Ken-
tucky, or on the frontier, where, from being a
dominant caste, or from the immediate vicinity of
unpeopled wildernesses, the inhabitants live a
half nomad life, there are as fine, perhaps finer
specimens of men to be seen; but there is no-
where in all America, an agricultural population,
the members of which personally till the soil,
that has such thews and sinews, such a healthy
development, or such generally prolonged life,

as our much-abused " *Pennsylvania Dutchmen*."
To be plain, if some of our crotchetty, one-ideaed
dyspeptic, thin, cadaverous, New England brethren would emigrate to our German counties;
follow, for a generation or two, the open air life
of our German farmers; and, last of all, inter-
marry into our vigorous, anti-hypochondrical
German families, they would soon cease to die by
such scores of consumption, to complain that
there were no longer any healthy women left, and
to amuse sensible people with such silly vagaries
of Pantheism, or a thousand and one intellectual
vagaries which are born of their abnormal physi-
cal condition."

GENERAL INDEX.

JUST ISSUED!

AN ACCOUNT

OF THE

MANNERS

OF THE

GERMAN INHABITANTS

OF PENNSYLVANIA.

WRITTEN 1789,

BY

BENJAMIN RUSH, M. D.

NOTES ADDED BY

Prof. I. DANIEL RUPP.

———————

To place this graphic Account of the Manners of the German Inhabitants of Pennsylvania, within the reach of all their numerous descendants, on the receipt of Fifty cents, a copy of it will be sent by mail postage prepaid.

A Liberal discount allowed to the trade.

SAMUEL P. TOWN, PUBLISHER,

614 CHESTNUT STREET,

Philadelphia, Pa.

Will be published by subscription, in 1876:

An Original Historical Narrative of Events, Incidents and Casualties in the early French, German and Swiss Settlements, in North America, prior to 1776.

With an Appendix.

BY

Prof. I. DANIEL RUPP,

Author of several Historical Works.

Metalmark Books is a joint imprint of The Pennsylvania State University
Press and the Office of Digital Scholarly Publishing at The Pennsylvania State
University Libraries. The facsimile editions published under this
imprint are reproductions of out-of-print, public domain works that hold
a significant place in Pennsylvania's rich literary and cultural past.
Metalmark editions are primarily reproduced from the University Libraries'
extensive Pennsylvania collections and in cooperation with other
state libraries. These volumes are available to the public for viewing online
and can be ordered as print-on-demand paperbacks.

LIBRARY OF CONGRESS CATALOGING-IN-PUBLICATION DATA

Rush, Benjamin, 1746–1813
An account of the manners of the German inhabitants of Pennsylvania,
written 1789 / Benjamin Rush.
p.   cm.
Includes index.
Summary: "A description, originally published in 1789, of Pennsylvania
German culture. Reprint of 1875 edition, with notes, preface, and appendixes
by Pennsylvania historian Daniel Rupp"—Provided by publisher.
ISBN 978-0-271-04884-0 (pbk. : alk. paper)
1. Pennsylvania Dutch.
I. Rupp, I. Daniel (Israel Daniel), 1803–1878.
II. Title.

F160.G3R8 2011
305.893'10748—dc22
2010053168

Printed in the United States of America
Reprinted 2011 by The Pennsylvania State University Press
University Park, PA 16802-1003